ABRAHAM LINCOLN

The 16th President

by Josh Gregory

Consultant: Meena Bose
Director, Peter S. Kalikow Center for the Study of the American Presidency
Peter S. Kalikow Chair in Presidential Studies
Professor, Political Science
Hofstra University
Hempstead, New York

BEARPORT
PUBLISHING

New York, New York

Credits

Cover, © dbimages/Alamy; 4, Courtesy of the Library of Congress; 5, Courtesy of the Library of Congress; 6, National Park Service; 7, Courtesy of the Library of Congress; 8, © North Wind Picture Archives/Alamy; 9T, © North Wind Picture Archives/Alamy; 9B, © The Design Lab; 10, © The Design Lab; 11L, Courtesy of the Library of Congress; 11R, © Glasshouse Images/Alamy; 12, Courtesy of the Library of Congress; 13, Courtesy of the Library of Congress; 14–15, © North Wind Picture Archives/Alamy; 16, Courtesy of the Library of Congress; 17, Courtesy of the Library of Congress; 18, © Anthony Correia/Shutterstock.com; 19T, © Jason Patrick Ross/Shutterstock.com; 19B, © Pete Spiro/Shutterstock.com; 20L, National Park Service; 20R, Courtesy of the Library of Congress; 21TL, Courtesy of the Library of Congress; 21TR, Courtesy of the Library of Congress; 21B, Courtesy of the Library of Congress; 22, © Sandy Stupart/Shutterstock.com; 23T, Courtesy of the Library of Congress; 23C, © Anthony Correia/Shutterstock.com; 23B, © North Wind Picture Archives/Alamy.

Publisher: Kenn Goin
Editor: Jessica Rudolph
Creative Director: Spencer Brinker
Design: The Design Lab
Photo Researcher: Jennifer Zeiger

Special thanks to fifth-grader Lucy Barr and second-grader Brian Barr for their help in reviewing this book.

Library of Congress Cataloging-in-Publication Data

Gregory, Josh.
  Abraham Lincoln: the 16th President / by Josh Gregory.
      pages cm. — (A first look at America's Presidents)
  Includes bibliographical references and index.
  Audience: Ages 5–8.
  ISBN 978-1-62724-554-8 (library binding) — ISBN 1-62724-554-5 (library binding)
  1. Lincoln, Abraham, 1809–1865—Juvenile literature. 2. Presidents—United States—Biography—Juvenile literature.
  I. Title.
  E457.905.G76 2015
  973.7092—dc23
  [B]

                                        2014034605

For more information, write to Bearport Publishing Company, Inc., 45 West 21st Street, Suite 3B, New York, New York 10010. Printed in the United States of America.

10 9 8 7 6 5 4 3 2 1

CONTENTS

A Great Leader 4

Farm Boy 6

Speaking Against Slavery 8

Becoming President 10

A Country at War 12

The War Ends 14

The Death of the President . . . 16

Remembering Lincoln 18

Timeline 20

Facts and Quotes 22

Glossary 23

Index 24

Read More 24

Learn More Online 24

About the Author 24

A Great Leader

Abraham Lincoln was a great leader. During his time as president, the United States was torn apart. Northern states and Southern states were fighting each other. Lincoln helped keep the country together.

Battles took place across the United States while Lincoln was president.

Abraham Lincoln was the 16th president. He served from 1861 to 1865.

Lincoln is remembered as one of the greatest presidents in U.S. history.

5

Farm Boy

Abraham Lincoln was born in Kentucky in 1809. His family was poor. As a boy, Abraham helped with farmwork. He also loved to read.

Abraham grew up in a log cabin in Kentucky much like this one.

Abraham taught himself many things by reading.

Sometimes Abraham would walk for miles to borrow a book from another family.

Speaking Against Slavery

When he was 21 years old, Abraham Lincoln moved to Illinois. He became a lawyer there. He also made speeches saying that **slavery** was wrong. Slavery was against the law in Northern states, but it was allowed in Southern states.

Lincoln was a skillful speaker.

Arctic Ocean

United States

Pacific Ocean

AFRICA

Atlantic Ocean

Indian Ocean

Southern Ocean

N W E S

For hundreds of years, people had been kidnapped from their homes in Africa. They were brought to the United States as slaves.

Millions of slaves worked on farms in the South.

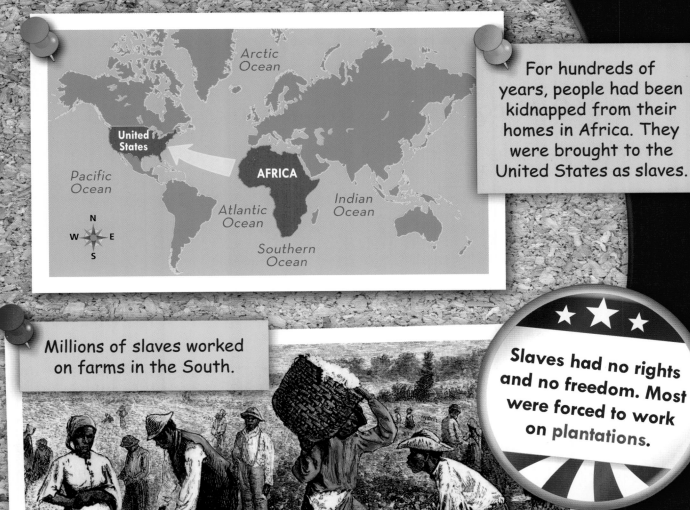

Slaves had no rights and no freedom. Most were forced to work on plantations.

9

Becoming President

In 1860, Lincoln ran for president and won. Many people in Southern states did not want him as their leader. They wanted to keep slavery. They broke off from the rest of the country. Then, in 1861, the Northern and Southern states went to war against each other.

This map shows the Northern and Southern states that went to war.

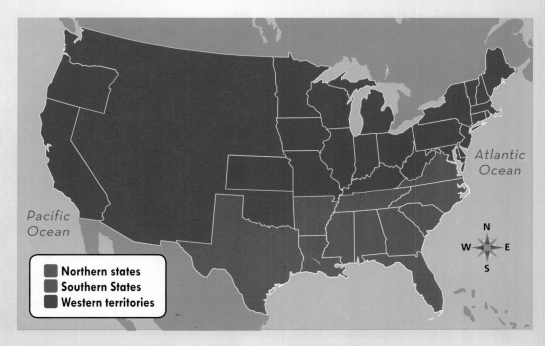

Pacific Ocean

Atlantic Ocean

Northern states
Southern States
Western territories

The war fought between the North and the South is called the Civil War.

Southern soldiers were called Confederate troops.

Northern soldiers were called Union troops.

A Country at War

Lincoln led the Northern states during the war. It was a terrible time for the country. Many soldiers died. Lincoln gave speeches to help people understand the importance of the fight.

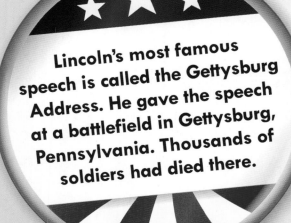

Lincoln's most famous speech is called the Gettysburg Address. He gave the speech at a battlefield in Gettysburg, Pennsylvania. Thousands of soldiers had died there.

Lincoln wrote the Gettysburg Address himself. He delivered it in 1863.

About 750,000 soldiers died during the Civil War.

The War Ends

In 1865, the North won the war. The United States was one country again. Many people celebrated.

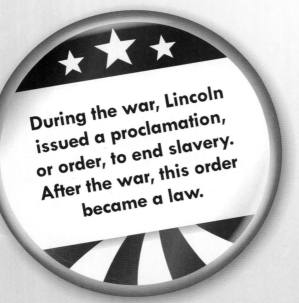

During the war, Lincoln issued a proclamation, or order, to end slavery. After the war, this order became a law.

Americans cheered as Northern soldiers
returned home after the war.

The Death of the President

People's happiness did not last long, however. One night in 1865, Lincoln went to see a play. There was a loud bang! A man inside the theater had shot him. He was angry that the South had lost the war. The next morning, Lincoln died.

John Wilkes Booth shot Lincoln in a theater in Washington, D.C.

A train took Lincoln's body back to Illinois. Millions of people came out to say good-bye to the president.

Remembering Lincoln

Today, we remember Lincoln in many ways. His picture is on the penny and the five-dollar bill. His face is carved into Mount Rushmore. Many towns and cities are named after him.

Each year, millions of people visit the Lincoln Memorial in Washington, D.C.

Mount Rushmore includes the faces of George Washington, Thomas Jefferson, Theodore Roosevelt, and Abraham Lincoln.

Lincoln

IN GOD WE TRUST

LIBERTY

2010

Lincoln's face is on the front of every penny.

Here are some major events from Abraham Lincoln's life.

1809
Abraham Lincoln is born in Kentucky.

1830
Lincoln moves to Illinois.

◄────── 1800 ────── 1810 ────── 1820 ────── 1830 ──────

1816
Lincoln's family moves to Indiana.

1834
Lincoln is elected to the Illinois State Legislature.

1847–1849
Lincoln serves as a member of the U.S. Congress.

1860
Lincoln is elected president of the United States.

1863
Lincoln gives his most famous speech, the Gettysburg Address.

| 1840 | 1850 | 1860 | 1870 |

1861
The Civil War begins.

1864
Lincoln is re-elected president.

1865
The Civil War ends. Lincoln is killed. Slavery is outlawed in all states.

FACTS and QUOTES

"If slavery is not wrong, nothing is wrong."

Lincoln was the tallest president—at six feet, four inches (1.9 m).

Lincoln liked to tell funny stories and jokes. This helped him make friends easily.

"Those who deny freedom to others deserve it not for themselves."

"A house divided against itself cannot stand."

Lincoln married Mary Todd. They had four children: Eddie, Willie, Tad, and Robert. Only Robert lived to be an adult.

EMANCIPATION

GLOSSARY

Civil War (SIV-uhl WOR) the war that took place from 1861 to 1865 between the Northern and the Southern states

memorial (muh-MOR-ee-uhl) a statue or other object made to help people remember someone

plantations (plan-TAY-shuhnz) large farms where crops such as cotton are grown

slavery (SLAY-vur-ee) the practice of forcing people to work with no pay and not allowing them to come and go freely

Index

Booth, John Wilkes 16
childhood 6–7
Civil War 4, 10–11,
    12–13, 14–15, 16, 21
education 7
elections 10, 20–21
five-dollar bill 18

Gettysburg Address 12,
    21
Illinois 8, 17, 20
Kentucky 6, 20
law career 8
Lincoln, Mary Todd 22
Lincoln Memorial 18

Mount Rushmore 18–19
penny 18–19
slavery 8–9, 10, 14, 21, 22
soldiers 11, 12–13, 15
speeches 8, 12, 21
U.S. Congress 21
Washington, D.C. 16, 18

Read More

Gilpin, Caroline Crosson. *Abraham Lincoln (National Geographic Readers).* Washington, DC: National Geographic (2012).

Kalman, Maira. *Looking at Lincoln.* New York: Nancy Paulsen Books (2012).

Meltzer, Brad. *I Am Abraham Lincoln (Ordinary People Change the World).* New York: Dial Books for Young Readers (2014).

Learn More Online

To learn more about Abraham Lincoln, visit **www.bearportpublishing.com/AmericasPresidents**

About the Author: Josh Gregory writes and edits books for kids. He lives in Chicago, Illinois.